W9-DFE-061

WITHDRAWN

Coasts in Danger

Earth Alert!

Polly Goodman

Gareth Stevens
Publishing

Please visit our website, www.garethstevens.com.
For a free color catalogue of all our high-quality books,
call toll free 1-800-542-2595 or fax 1-877-542-2596.

Library of Congress Cataloging-in-Publication Data

Goodman, Polly.
Coasts in danger / Polly Goodman.
     p. cm.— (Earth alert)
Includes index.
ISBN 978-1-4339-5996-7 (library binding)
1. Coasts—Environmental aspects. 2. Coast changes. 3. Coastal ecology. I.
Title.
GB454.G66 2011
333.91'7—dc22

2010049255

This edition first published in 2012 by
Gareth Stevens Publishing
111 East 14th Street, Suite 349
New York, NY 10003

Copyright © 2012 Wayland/Gareth Stevens Publishing

Editorial Director: Kerri O'Donnell
Design Director: Haley Harasymiw

Printed in China

CPSIA compliance information. Batch WAS11GS. For further information contact Gareth Stevens, New York, New York at 1-800-542-2595

Picture acknowledgements
Cover: Shutterstock; Aerofilms Limited 7; Axiom
Photographic Agency (Jim Holmes) 25; Chapel Studios (Zul Mukhida) 6; James Davis Travel
Photography 10, 17; Ecoscene (Wayne Lawler) 13; Robert Estall Photo Library 18; Eye Ubiquitous (Tim
Hawkins) 1, (M. Allwood-Coppin) 3, 8–9, (Pauline Thorn ton) 5, (Bob Gibbons) 8, (Paul Seheult) 26,
(Paul Thompson) 28; Getty Images (Art Wolfe) 4–5, (David Olsen) 19, (Nigel Press) 20, (David
Woodfall) 21; Horsehead Wetlands Center, 27 (both); Impact Photos (Javed A Jafferji) 12, (Simon
Grosset) 14, (Mark Henley) 15, (Piers Cavendish) 21; RSPB Images 11; Topham
Picturepoint 16, 24; Cozyta/Shutterstock 22, Tannen Maury/Corbis 23.

Contents

What Are Coasts?   4

Animals and Plants   8

People and Coasts   12

Threats   18

Protecting Coasts   26

Glossary   30

Topic Web and Further Resources   31

Index   32

What Are Coasts?

Coasts are areas of land next to the sea. They are important places. Most of the world's people live on or near coasts. Coasts are also home to many different plants and animals.

Coasts have different natural shapes. Bays and beaches have formed where the sea has worn away soft rock. Where there is harder rock, steep cliffs have formed.

A long beach on an island in the Pacific Ocean. ↻

Rivers at Coasts

Where rivers meet the sea, they form estuaries or deltas.

An estuary is a place where a river meets the sea. The tides go in and out, covering and uncovering land in an estuary.

Deltas are flat, triangular areas of land near a coast, where a river splits into many channels. They form as rivers reach the sea, dropping fine mud, called silt, on the land.

TIDES

Tides are the rise and fall of the sea. They are controlled by the moon.

High tide is when the water is at its highest point on the shore.

Low tide is when the water is at its lowest point.

Some plants and birds can live on steep cliffs like this one.

Changing Coasts

Coasts are always changing. Strong waves and winds constantly wear away rocks. Whole beaches can be washed away by storms.

Some bays gradually fill up with silt dropped by rivers. The bays get more and more shallow until new land is formed. However, the fastest changes to coasts are made by people.

↷ This beach is being worn away by waves and the wind.

Activity

YOUR COAST

Look at a map of the United States, and find out where the nearest coast is. If you live near a coast, measure the distance from your school. Then describe the coastal region, using the Internet to get information if you need to:

* Is there a beach or cliffs?
* Is there a village, town, or city on the coast?
* What types of boats arrive at the coast?
* Are there roads or railroads along the coast?

TRUE STORY

A TOWN UNDER THE SEA

Dunwich is a small village in Suffolk, on the east coast of the UK. It used to be the tenth largest town in England. But today, most of the old town is under the sea.

In the eleventh century, Dunwich had many houses and large churches. By the fourteenth century, waves had begun washing away the cliffs at the edge of the town. Houses and other buildings fell into the sea.

Now the coast at Dunwich is half a mile (800 m) farther inland than it used to be.

The ruins at the bottom of the photo are the only buildings left from the old town of Dunwich. ◑

Animals and Plants

Coasts are important places for many plants and animals. For some, coasts are permanent homes. For others, they are just resting places.

Seabirds spend much of their time catching fish in the sea. But in between fishing trips, many rest on the shore. Some seabirds raise their young on the shore, and feed them with fish.

◑ **Sea lions on the Galapagos Islands.**

The Shoreline

The shoreline is the area between high and low tide. Plants and animals that live there are specially suited to living both in and out of the water.

When the tides go out, shellfish such as mussels and oysters attach themselves tightly onto rocks. Their hard shells protect their bodies from drying out.

Shorelines provide a feast for birds when the tides go out. Where mudflats and rock pools are uncovered, birds can pluck out insects and fish with their beaks.

RICH PICKINGS FOR BIRDS

One cubic yard of mud in an estuary provides birds with as much energy as there is in 12 chocolate candy bars!

Seabirds called gannets rest on the shore in South Africa. ↻

9

River Estuaries

Estuaries are broad mouths of rivers where salt water from the sea meets the fresh river water. The water in estuaries rises and falls as the tides wash in and out.

Estuaries are home to lots of different plants and animals. Plants grow easily in the shallow water because the sunlight they need can reach the bottom.

⟲ Fish called mustard rays in a mangrove swamp in Ecuador.

Natural Cleaners

Some plants in estuaries are natural cleaners. Beds of reeds purify water for plants and animals. They even clean water polluted by people, so that it does not harm the environment.

REST STOPS

Estuaries and beaches provide ideal resting places for migrating birds.

Sanderlings are birds that breed in the Arctic. At the end of the short summer, food runs out, so the sanderlings have to spend the winter somewhere else. They fly south, all the way to the coast of West Africa. The following spring they fly back to the Arctic.

The journey is too far to make without stopping. The sanderlings rest on beaches and estuaries along the way. If these areas are built over by people, the birds will lose their feeding grounds and starve.

◑ **Sanderlings on a beach.**

People and Coasts

Coasts have always been very important places for people. They provide food from the sea and from the land. They are also used for transportation and trade.

LIVING NEAR THE COAST

Half of the world's people live within 60 miles (100 km) of the sea.

Fish

People have hunted fish at sea for thousands of years. There are still important fishing ports on many coasts.

Fish are also farmed in ponds and tanks. Fish farming is big business on many coasts today because tons of fish can be produced and sold.

In cold countries, salmon are grown in tanks in the sea water. In some warm countries, fish ponds are made in mangrove forests but this can harm the environment.

⟳ **Fishermen putting out a net to catch fish.**

SHRIMP FARMING IN ECUADOR

Shrimp breed in the sea near the coast of Ecuador, in South America. But people make more money by raising the fish in large ponds along the coast. When the ponds are made, large areas of mangrove trees are cleared away.

After a few years, the ponds fill up with waste from the shrimp. They are so crowded that many shrimp catch diseases and die. New ponds are dug farther along the coast. This destroys more mangrove trees, and uses up natural places where fish breed.

◑ A fish pond in Ecuador.

Farming on Land

Flat land near coasts is good for farming crops and animals. The soil in river deltas is very fertile, because when the river floods, it leaves rich mud on the land around it.

In the Netherlands, new farmland has been made near coasts. Walls, called dikes, have been built around land that is uncovered at low tide. The walls keep out the sea, and ditches drain water away.

Farmland on the coast of New Zealand. ↻

Transportation and Trade

Before airplanes were invented, people traveled between countries by ship. So coasts were important places for transportation and trade.

Because coasts were good trading places, many settlements grew up there. Cities such as New York, Sydney, and Tokyo grew up in natural harbors. These protected ships from strong winds and waves.

Many natural harbors are now busy ports, with factories and warehouses, airports and roads, offices and houses. Bulky goods such as coal and oil are loaded and unloaded there from big ships.

↻ A busy port in Hong Kong.

First Homes

In the past, when explorers or settlers went to new countries, the first places they came to were coasts. In the 1500s, Europeans sailed to North and South America and settled on the coasts before they moved inland.

In the nineteenth and twentieth centuries, millions of people migrated, or moved to new countries to live. For example, people moved from Europe to the United States, and from the UK to Australia. Many people did not move away from the coasts where they first arrived.

People arriving in the UK from the Caribbean in 1958. ⊙

Tourism

Coasts are good tourist attractions because people can do lots of different activities, such as swimming, windsurfing, or kitesurfing.

Many coasts also have blue seas, sandy beaches, and coral reefs for people to enjoy. Many people fly thousands of miles to visit coasts in other countries.

◉ A beach in Hawaii.

Activity

TOURISM SURVEY

1. Get a vacation guide from a travel agent and choose another state or country.

2. Find the vacation destinations listed in the guide, on a map. (The guide will probably have a map in it.)

* Where are most of the vacations?
* How would you travel to the place?
* How far away is it?

Threats

People are damaging coasts around the world. Sometimes it is hard to see the damage we do, especially if it happens slowly over a long time.

Areas of coast that might look like wasteland are usually home to many plants and animals. They may also do an important job. Sand dunes and cliffs protect the land from flooding when there are high tides or storms. Reed beds clean our water.

Many plants and animals depend on this river estuary. ↻

New Buildings

New building projects for local people or tourist resorts change a coast forever. Plants and animals lose their habitat. Fish lose their breeding grounds. The area may lose its natural defenses against flooding. The new buildings and stores may create pollution and garbage. They can also destroy an area's natural beauty.

⌒ A marina in San Diego, California, with boats, shops, offices, and homes.

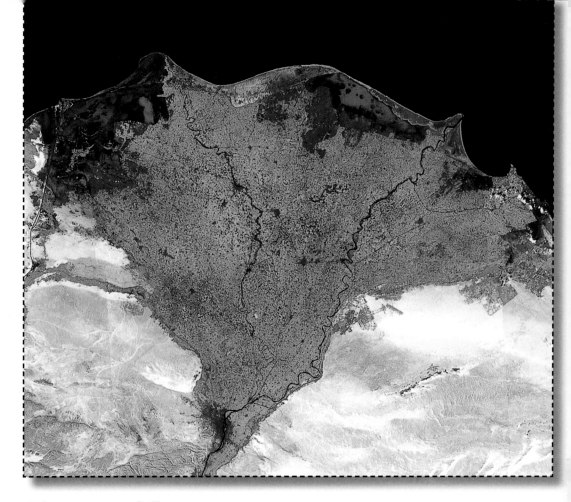

This satellite photograph (taken from space) shows the huge delta of the Nile River, in Egypt. ⮌

Rivers and Dams

Activities inland can also damage coasts. Pollution from factories and farms may flow into rivers and be carried down to the coast. Water pollution can kill plants and animals in estuaries.

Dams change the natural flow of rivers. They can stop rivers carrying silt to deltas, so the soil in deltas becomes less fertile. Then farmers in deltas find it harder to grow food.

Dams can also stop nutrients being carried down to estuaries by rivers, so newborn fish have less food. If fewer fish breed in estuaries, there are fewer fish at sea for us to catch and eat.

Pollution

Many coasts have been damaged by pollution. One kind of pollution is sewage. In many parts of the world, sewage is pumped straight into the sea without being treated first. The sea can only break down small amounts of sewage. So in these places the water around coasts is polluted.

Sewage in the water around coasts is unpleasant and unhealthy. The sewage can poison shellfish and other animals that grow near the shore. People who swim or surf in the water may get sick.

Sewage washed up on a swimming beach. ◒

Chemicals

Chemicals used in homes, offices, factories, and farms are washed into the sea by rivers. They pollute the water, killing plants and animals and destroying their habitat.

GARBAGE

Garbage and pollution dropped on coasts can be carried thousands of miles away. The garbage below was found on Ducie Atoll. This is a group of islands in the South Pacific where there are no people. The nearest place where people live is 3,100 miles (5,000 km) away.

* 171 glass bottles from 15 countries
* 113 sea markers
* 74 bottle tops
* 25 shoes
* 14 crates
* 7 soft drink cans
* 6 light tubes
* 1 toy airplane
* 2 dolls' heads
* 2 ballpoint pen tops

⋂ Garbage piled up on a beach.

OIL SPILL IN THE GULF OF MEXICO

In April 2010, a fire broke out on a deep-water rig that was drilling for oil in the Gulf of Mexico. The rig sank. Vast amounts of oil started to gush from the broken head of the oil well.

It took about three months to stop the leak. After many attempts, BP, the oil company, managed to block the oil flow with a cap on the well. But the oil spread and washed up on the Gulf Coast states. It was a disaster for sea life, killing birds, fish, shellfish, and sea turtles.

⋔ Brown pelicans waiting to be cleaned of oil after the Gulf oil spill, which was the biggest in U.S. history.

Climate Change

Most scientists believe the world's climate is changing. People have caused the problem by burning fossil fuels, such as coal, gas, and oil, to make electricity and run machines. When fossil fuels are burned, they release gases into the atmosphere. These gases slowly raise the world's temperature.

As the climate grows warmer, huge areas of ice in the Arctic and Antarctic are likely to melt. Sea levels will rise because of the melting ice and the warming ocean water. As it heats up, it expands. Areas near coasts will floc more easily and some islands will be covered in water.

Melting icebergs in the Antarctic. ↻

In a warmer climate, many homes become at risk from flooding. Countries with low coasts, such as the Netherlands and Bangladesh, will have to build expensive walls to protect against floods.

Mudflats and estuaries could become permanently covered by water. This would destroy the habitat for plants and animals. Wildlife that couldn't adapt quickly enough would die out.

⌒ Floods are already common in Bangladesh.

Activity

EXPANDING WATER

Find out how water expands as it warms up.

1. Half fill an empty squeezable ketchup bottle with water at room temperature and add food coloring.
2. Push a straw in the bottle until it goes under the surface of the water. Seal the gap around the straw tightly with modeling clay.
3. Blow air in the straw so the water level rises 2 in. (5 cm) above the bottle top. Mark level.
4. Put the bottle next to a radiator. What happens to the water level?

Protecting Coasts

Coasts are important places for people, plants, and animals. But it is easy for people to spoil coasts, especially if they do not realize how important they are.

U.S. WETLANDS

When a wetland area is destroyed for building, another wetland area is created to make up for the loss.

Many countries are trying to make more people understand how important coasts are. Information centers and bulletin boards display information about the different plants and animals that live along a coast. Tourists are asked to help take care of beaches.

⟲ This sign in Thailand asks tourists not to stand on coral or drop litter in the sea.

CHESAPEAKE BAY

Chesapeake Bay is a large estuary on the east coast of the United States. Many rivers flow into the bay and it is home to hundreds of species of wildlife and thousands of types of plants.

⌒ Children at the visitors' center.

Since 1976, there has been a program to protect the bay. The organizers work with the local government, farmers, and residents to reduce water pollution. They restore habitats for fish, birds, and other animals. Also, they aim to stop overfishing in the bay.

Students study the wildlife in the bay, as part of the Chesapeake Bay education program. ⮕

Conservation

Many coastal areas are being turned into conservation areas or nature reserves. New building projects are not allowed, and the areas are kept as natural as possible.

Nature reserves are usually beautiful places where visitors can watch wildlife. Visitors have to follow certain rules, so they do not disturb the wildlife.

In some countries, before new building projects can go ahead, scientists make a study of the area. They give advice about how to construct the building so that it does not cause too much damage.

Coastlines like this one need to be protected so that visitors do not damage them. ⟲

Activity

Look at this Drawing of a Coastline

1. List the natural things you can see, such as beaches and cliffs.

2. List the different jobs people could do, such as fishing.

3. Which areas could be made into conservation areas?

Glossary

Conservation Taking care of a natural area or material to save it for the future.

Defenses Materials that protect against damage or attack.

Environment Everything in our surroundings: the earth, air, and water.

Estuaries Places where a river meets the sea.

Fertile Something that is rich and productive.

Flood When a large amount of water covers land that is usually dry.

Habitat The natural home of a plant or animal.

Migrating Moving from one place to another.

Nutrients Things that feed plants, animals, and people.

Overfishing Taking so many fish from the sea that the number becomes very low.

Pollution Damage to air, water, and land by harmful materials.

Ports Places where ships stop to load or unload people or goods.

Rig A large piece of equipment for taking oil or gas out of the bottom of the sea.

Settlers People who go to a new place to live.

Sewage Liquid waste that is carried away from homes.

Shoreline The area of the shore between high and low tide.

Tides The rise and fall of the sea on the shore.

Wetlands Areas of low land that are covered by shallow water for much of the year.

Further Information

MUSIC
- Coastal sounds: birds, waves, ships
- Music associated with coasts, such as *Fingal's Cave*

GEOGRAPHY
- Landforms and processes
- Human use of coasts
- Land reclamation
- Nature conservation
- Environmental issues: global climate change and sea level, tourism, overfishing, pollution
- Population topics

HISTORY
- Migrations of people and religions
- Changes of coasts over time

ARTS & CRAFTS
- Using coasts as a stimulus for drawing, painting, and modeling

Topic Web

DESIGN AND TECHNOLOGY
- Coastal building or defenses
- Land reclamation
- Pollution control

MATH
- Measuring angles of slopes, the length of coasts, or the height of cliffs
- Simple statistics

SCIENCE
- Ecosystems
- Biodiversity
- Adaptation to environment
- Ecological niches
- Food chains
- Environmental issues: e.g. habitat loss, water pollution, climate change

ENGLISH
- Using coasts as a stimulus for creative writing
- Appropriate poetry
- Library skills

Books

Landform Top Tens: The World's Most Amazing Coasts by Anna Claybourne (Heinemann-Raintree, 2009)

Gulf Coast Oil Spill: Poor Little Pelican + A KidReport Photo-Documentary by Carole Marsh (Gallopade International, 2010)

The Burgess Seashore Book for Children by Thornton W. Burgess (Dover, 2005)

Where People Live: Living at the Coast by Neil Morris (Smart Apple Media, 2004)

Websites

Exploring Estuaries
http://water.epa.gov/learn/kids/estuaries/index.cfm
Discovery estuaries, including virtual tours and activities.

U.S. National Park Service
www.nps.gov/index.htm
Type in your local coastline for website links and activities.

Coastal Care
http://coastalcare.org/educate/
Links and activities with information about caring for coastal and beach habitats.

Index

animals 4, 8, 9, 10, 14, 18, 19, 20, 21, 22, 23, 25, 27
Antarctic 24
Arctic 11, 24
Australia 15, 16

Bangladesh 25
beaches 4, 6, 11, 17, 22, 26
birds 5, 8, 9, 11, 23, 27

Caribbean 16
Chesapeake Bay 27
cliffs 4, 5, 7, 18
climate 24–5
conservation 27, 28, 29

dams 20
deltas 5, 14, 20
Ducie Atoll 22
Dunwich 7

Ecuador 10, 13
Egypt 20
estuaries 5, 9, 10, 11, 18, 20, 25, 27
Europe 16

farms 14, 20, 27

fish 8, 9, 10, 12, 20, 23, 27
fish farms 12, 13
fishing 12, 27
floods 14, 18, 19, 24, 25
food 12, 20
fuels 24

Galapagos Islands 8

habitats 19, 22, 25, 27
harbors 15
Hawaii 17
Hong Kong 15

Japan 15, 21

Netherlands 14, 25
New York 15
New Zealand 14

oil spill 23

Pacific Ocean 4
people 4, 6, 10, 11, 12, 13, 14, 15, 16, 17, 18, 19, 21, 24, 25, 26, 27, 28, 29
plants 4, 5, 8, 9, 10, 14, 18, 19, 20, 22, 25, 27

pollution 10, 19, 20, 21, 22, 23, 27, 30
ports 12, 15

reeds 10, 18
rivers 5, 10, 20

sanderlings 11
settlers 16
sewage 21
shoreline 9
shrimp 13
South Africa 9
Sydney 15

Thailand 26
tides 5, 9, 10, 18
Tokyo 15
tourism 17, 19, 21, 26
trade 12, 15
transportation 12, 15

UK 7, 16
United States 15, 16, 19, 23, 26, 27

wetlands 26